Living with

Grief

By Stephen J. Carter

SAINT LOUIS

Jane Fryar, Project Editor
Thomas J. Doyle and Roger Sonnenberg, Series Editors
Cindi Crismon, Assistant to the Editors

Your comments and suggestions concerning this material are
solicited. Please write to Product Manager, Youth and Adult Bible
Studies, Concordia Publishing House, 3558 S. Jefferson Ave., St.
Louis, MO, 63118-3968.

Contents

About the Author

Stephen Carter shares his experience with the grieving process through the illness and death of his 23-year-old daughter, Becky. Becky, a champion gymnast and university honors graduate, struggled with aplastic anemia for three and a half years before dying in Seattle from complications of a bone marrow transplant. Steve and his wife Gail, son Mark, and other daughter Amy continue to struggle with the painful loss of Becky while at the same time trusting in the promises of God through Jesus Christ. The Carter family received tremendous support from the Christian community, as well as a listening ear from those who also grieve the loss of a son or daughter.

Prior to becoming president of Concordia Publishing House, Dr. Carter served CPH as executive vice-president. He also served for fifteen years as a local church pastor and for five years as a seminary professor. He has authored *My Daily Devotion*, a devotional annual, and books on marriage enrichment, team ministry, and continuing education for pastors.

Grief: Facing Your Loss

Focusing Our Sights

In this first session we will begin to explore grief and the grieving process by describing the loss of our loved one. We will identify myths commonly held by Christians about grief and observe the grief expressed in the story of Lazarus' death. Finally, we will be led to the comfort and hope God provides through Christ.

Focusing Our Attention

Becky was such a vital, vibrant daughter—champion gymnast, cheerleader, inquisitive student, always on the move with church and social activities, full of dreams for marriage and a high school teaching career. Now she is dead, lying motionless in a Seattle hospital intensive care room, 2,500 miles from home.

We had struggled and prayed with her for three and a half years—ever since that fateful day when the doctor announced during a routine physical checkup that Becky had a serious blood problem, later diagnosed as aplastic anemia. The fight for life was on.

Instead of preparing for her junior year at the university as she had planned, she stayed

5

home for endless tests and treatments designed to get her bone marrow working again. Our hopes were raised and then dashed many times over. Medicines worked and then caused serious side effects. Additional treatments hurt more but didn't help much. Blood transfusions multiplied.

We grieved with her at the loss of things dear to her heart, like her college gymnastics career and the opportunity to study in Cambridge, England. Still, through the trials, Becky received strength from God's Word as the Holy Spirit renewed her trust in her Savior.

She did manage to return to school later and to graduate with her class. She participated in her sister's and brother's weddings. She reached out to hurting friends and found opportunities to witness of God's love. She met a young man who asked her to marry him.

All the while, her physical condition worsened until only one medical hope remained, a bone marrow transplant from an unrelated donor. Supported by her family, fiancé, and friends from around the country who were praying for her, Becky drove with us to Seattle for an arduous procedure—one last chance for healing. God provided a perfectly matched bone marrow donor, one out of 600,000 names in the national registry. Once again we joined in prayers for her healing.

After three and a half weeks as an outpatient, Becky received the priceless bone marrow on December 18, a week before Christmas. We waited anxiously for the results. Becky's brother and sister joined us as we celebrated Christmas in Seattle and continued visiting her in isolation. Then complications arose from the chemotherapy. Just as the new bone marrow *was beginning to work, liver and kidney disease sapped her strength.*

On January 9, 22 days after the transplant, Becky died. She was 23. Our hearts broke as we faced the reality of her death. She was with Jesus by His grace, but we felt alone without her.

1. What touches you about Becky's story?

2. In what ways would her death affect her parents, fiancé, brother, and sister?

Focusing on the Issue

Death enters our lives at different times in different ways. We are almost never prepared. A grandparent or aunt. Dad or mom. A dear friend. A brother or sister. Husband or wife.

Death comes suddenly through an accident or heart attack. Death creeps up on us through a lingering illness or debilitating cancer. We may live for years without any intimate contact with death and then face a series of losses in a short time. Or we may experience the death of someone close to us at an early age and continue to lose loved ones at regular intervals. Our own death is always before us.

❖

How do we learn to face death? We may observe how other people handle the loss of a loved one. We may read books about grief and loss. We hear sermons about death. We read what the Bible has to say about it. Consciously or unconsciously, we learn.

Valuable as this process of information gathering can be, sometimes we develop myths about how Christians grieve. These myths can stand in the way of a healthy grief process. For example:

Myth 1: If your faith is strong enough, you won't grieve. After all, Jesus Christ rose from the grave on the third day. The Bible promises us eternal life in heaven through faith in Jesus. So the feelings associated with grief aren't that important.

Myth 2: If your faith is strong enough, you will get over grief as quickly as possible. It is acceptable to grieve at the time of death and at the funeral. But after that Christians should get hold of themselves and return to their normal lives. Don't let your grieving continue for too long.

Myth 3: If your faith is strong enough, you will control your emotions. Don't let your sorrow and hopelessness overwhelm you. Don't express anger. Don't let others know how upset you are. Witness your faith by being strong for others.

1. Which of these myths have you encountered? Can you think of others?

2. Have you yourself ever believed any of these myths? If so, what resulted from that belief?

3. Talk together with a partner or with your group about what makes each one a myth. What is the truth in each case?

Focusing on God's Word

Read **John 11.** As you do, note the ways each individual in the account experienced and expressed grief.

1. What grief responses can you identify? As you answer this question in the space below, also jot down the number of the verse in which you noted each response.

2. Which grief response(s) did Jesus rebuke? What do you deduce from this?

3. How did Jesus' relationship with this family make all the difference in the situation?

Focusing on My Life

You have never met Lazarus. Or Mary. Or Martha. You probably don't know Becky and her family. Nevertheless, if you have picked up this booklet and are working through it by yourself or in a group, you are almost certainly no stranger to the grief that comes when a loved one dies.

1. Take a few minutes right now to talk with one other person in your group. Briefly tell one another about the death of your loved one. Doubtless this will be painful for you and for the person who listens to your story. These guidelines will make the exercise somewhat easier:

a. Don't force yourself to share more than you can share comfortably.

b. For now, focus as much as you can on the external facts. If you can, describe your relationship, your loved one's age, and the circumstances of the death.

c. Be prepared for tears and let them fall if they come. Don't try to stuff feelings or tears back inside.

d. Your group's leader will let you know about the time allotted for each of you to tell your story. Keep the limitations in mind as you organize your telling.

e. When you're the listener, put your partner at ease. Don't offer advice. Don't take on responsibility for making your partner feel better. Don't comfort with platitudes (e.g., "I know just how you feel"; "Don't cry—you know your dad is in heaven now"). Simply listen with compassion.

2. If you could choose one word to describe your feelings as you think about the death of that loved one right now, what word would you choose?

a. Explain to your partner the word you chose and your reasons for choosing it.

b. Then listen while your partner does the same.

3. Has Jesus' relationship with you made any difference in your situation? If so, tell your partner a little about that difference. If not, feel free to say so. Then give your partner something specific you would like him or her to pray about for you this week (e.g., "Jesus feels so far away. Please pray that as I open my Bible, I would know He is with me." "I haven't been able to go to church since the death.

Please pray that God would give me courage and someone to sit with me.")

Focusing on the Week Ahead

1. Read **Psalm 73** several times, perhaps even once each day. This is a song Asaph wrote at a time of confusion in his own life. He went to God's house to sort out his thoughts and feelings. The psalm came out of that process. It never defines Asaph's original problem, perhaps so that each of us as God's people can keep our own losses and anxieties in mind as we meditate on Asaph's questions and his resolution.

2. Memorize **John 11:25–26.** Write it on a note card, post it where you will see it, and read it, often as you learn it.

Grief: The Cry of Pain

2

Focusing Our Sights

In this second session we will be introduced to what have been called the "five cries of grief." We will then focus on the cry of pain. We will look to the comfort and peace that only God's Word can provide as we seek to face our pain and apply God's healing.

Focusing Our Attention

My son Mark and I leave Becky's intensive care room. He's a possible platelet donor and we need to get his blood typed. While we wait in line, the phone rings. Becky's doctor says, "You better come back here immediately."

Heart in throat, we rush across the street to hear that Becky has suffered a massive hemorrhage, which has shut down her brain stem. Numbly I hear the doctor's words and prepare to say good-bye to Becky's lifeless form.

The next minutes and hours blur. Time with Becky and with the family. Tears. Hugs from the chaplain. Phone calls about funeral arrangements back home. The calls to Becky's sister and Gail's mom. The task of setting up flight reservations home.

As we arrive that night in the basement apartment in Seattle where we are staying, Gail and I find ourselves overwhelmed with grief. The pain is almost unbearable. I feel the ceiling and walls pressing in on me. I can barely breathe.

The claustrophobia descends again as our plane rolls away from the gate for the flight from Seattle to St. Louis. I want to stand up and scream, to kick, to flail my arms.

Becky is dead. Nothing will change it. The pain seems unbearable.

In the first few minutes or hours after the death of a loved one, many people experience numbness, which is gradually eaten away by the pain of loss.

1. Why do you suppose God built into us the ability to numb our emotions? How does it serve us?

2. What expressions of pain from the account above strike you as very familiar? Explain briefly.

Focusing on the Issue

Every person who looses a loved one faces an ongoing process of grief, a process unique to that person and to the circumstances of the death. Yet as researchers study grieving, they discover certain patterns that can help those who mourn understand the grief they are experiencing.

Perhaps you know of the work of Elisabeth Kubler-Ross, who studied the process of dying and summarized this process in stages, stages that have often also been applied to the grieving process—denial, anger, bargaining, depression, and acceptance.

Rather than using this model, I have chosen to organize the remaining sessions of this study around what Merton P. and A. Irene Strommen have called the "five cries of grief" in their book by the same title (San Francisco: Harper, 1993). The Strommens' 25-year-old son, David, died after being struck by lightening while he served as a youth counselor at a camp in the Colorado Rockies.

These "five cries" will guide us as we talk about the grieving process in the light of God's Word and promises:

The cry of pain
The cry of longing
The cry for supportive love
The cry for understanding
The cry for significance

As Kubler-Ross before them, the Strommens stress that these facets of grief do not occur in neat and predictable sequence. Instead, we can experience each at different times in the process and with varying intensity.

The cry of pain strikes with great intensity soon after the death and lasts for some time. It seems to lessen over time but can recur unexpectedly. Irene Strommen has described it in these words: "Something has been wrenched, ripped, torn out of me" (p. 11). Merton Strommen writes, "Sobs began deep in my inmost being and moved up my body, contorting it forward. Never before had I understood what it meant to be 'bent low in grief' " (p. 20).

1. As you have moved through the grief process so far, have you read or studied anything in an attempt to understand the process? If so, why did you do it? If not, why not?

2. When and why might information about the process of grief be helpful?

3. Intellectual understanding, while useful, has its limits when we walk the path of grief. Why do you think this is so?

Focusing on God's Word

Read **Lamentations 3:16–33.**

❖❖❖❖❖❖❖❖❖❖❖❖❖❖❖❖❖❖❖❖❖❖❖❖❖❖❖

He has broken my teeth with gravel; He has trampled me in the dust. I have been

❖❖

deprived of peace; I have forgotten what prosperity is. So I say, "My splendor is gone and all that I had hoped from the LORD."

I remember my affliction and my wandering, the bitterness and the gall. I well remember them, and my soul is downcast within me.

Yet this I call to mind and therefore I have hope: Because of the LORD's great love we are not consumed, for His compassions never fail. They are new every morning; great is your faithfulness.

I say to myself, "The LORD is my portion; therefore I will wait for Him." The LORD is good to those whose hope is in Him, to the one who seeks Him; it is good to wait quietly for the salvation of the LORD.

For men are not cast off by the Lord forever. Though He brings grief, He will show compassion, so great is His unfailing love. For He does not willingly bring affliction or grief to the children of men. **(Lamentations 3:16–33)**

1. Put brackets around the words that describe the pain of grief that Jeremiah felt.

2. Underline the words that tell how Jeremiah found comfort.

3. It seems as though faith and despair battle one another inside Jeremiah's heart. Does it surprise you that so great a prophet as Jeremiah would wrestle with so much pain during a time of grief? Explain.

Focusing on My Life

1. Look back at the words from Lamentations that you put in brackets. In what ways do Jeremiah's words describe your own cry of pain?

2. Look back at the words from Lamentations that you underlined. Talk with your partner about how the truths that comforted Jeremiah also comfort you.

3. Together with a partner, think a little more about the battle between faith and despair that raged inside Jeremiah's heart.

a. Has that battle raged inside your own heart during your time of grief? If so, tell your partner a bit about it.

b. Has that battle or its intensity surprised you? Explain.

c. If you fight that kind of battle, does it mean you've given up on God or that your faith is deficient?

d. How will your Lord help you win that battle?

4. Psalm 73:21–26 brought great comfort to me in the early days after Becky's death. Read these verses.

❖❖❖❖❖❖❖❖❖❖❖❖❖❖❖❖❖❖❖❖❖❖❖❖❖❖❖

> When my heart was grieved and my spirit embittered, I was senseless and ignorant; I was a brute beast before You.
>
> Yet I am always with You; You hold me by my right hand. You guide me with Your counsel, and afterward You will take me into glory.
>
> Whom have I in heaven but You? And earth has nothing I desire besides You. My flesh and my heart may fail, but God is the strength of my heart and my portion forever. (Psalm 73:21–26)

❖❖❖❖❖❖❖❖❖❖❖❖❖❖❖❖❖❖❖❖❖❖❖❖❖❖❖

a. How do these verses reassure you of God's ever-present help, even while you experience the pain of grief?

b. How has the cross of Jesus Christ sealed for us the promises our Lord makes in this psalm? See also **Isaiah 53:3–6.**

Focusing on the Week Ahead

1. Notice times when the pain of grief may seem to war against your ability to trust and hope in God. At those times, reread **Lamentations 3:16–33** or **Psalm 73:21–26.** Let the Holy Spirit comfort you with the assurance that He is with you to ease the pain and to bring you hope from the very throne of God, even in the darkest times.

2. Read **Romans 8:18–39.** You may want to memorize one or more verses from this passage that you find especially meaningful.

3

Grief: The Cry of Longing ❖

Focusing Our Sights

In this third session we will hear the cry of longing that belongs to the grief process, and explore the intensity of longing in our own experience. This longing for our loved one will be connected with our longing for life forever with our Savior, a longing which He Himself will fill by His grace.

Focusing Our Attention

Eighteen months and nineteen days after Becky's death, I feel a wave of grief rolling over me. This morning I went to the basement family room and read Becky's diary from the summer of 1991, one and a half years before she died.

Surrounded by memorabilia from the funeral, which Gail and I just now are rereading, organizing, and putting away, tears well up in my eyes. I had thought I was doing much better. After all the memories and anniversaries of the first year following her death, life seemed more normal and bearable. Yet in these last two weeks, the cry of longing has returned.

All kinds of things, small and large, trigger

the longing—seeing her picture with Greg moved from the family room wall to a coffee table, walking through a mall where she loved to shop, reaching out to a co-worker whose six-year-old daughter has just been diagnosed with a violent type of cancer. The grief surfaces with powerful intensity.

I loved Becky so much. She brought much joy and challenge into my life. We discussed so many deep issues together. Art. Literature. Theology. She raised many stimulating questions as she learned and grew. Dad learned from daughter many times.

I long for those times together ... when I find the anniversary card and note she sent Gail and me six months before her death ... when I hear a tape recording of a presentation she gave to a sorority and fraternity group regarding her illness and testifying to her faith ... when I watch a home video taken the weekend she graduated from college ... when I page through her neatly and creatively organized photo albums of her high school and college days.

Yes, the cry of longing continues months and years after Becky's death.

Based on this account and on your own experience, how would you describe the cry of longing to a friend?

❖

Focusing on the Issue

In *Five Cries of Grief,* Mert and Irene Strommen describe the cry of longing in these words: "[It] reflects a pervasive loneliness that comes from missing our son, who remains an integral part of our lives. The cry is an ongoing desire to maintain him in the present tense" (p. xii).

We live with the awareness of our loved one's life and death. Sometimes the pain is so great that we can't stand the memories. Other times we want to remember and savor the closeness. Always we long for the loved one to be alive with us so we can share life with one another.

1. What recent memories of your loved one fill you with a cry of longing?

2. How has your longing made you feel lonely?

3. What helps you feel close to your loved one?

❖

Focusing on God's Word

While we encounter the cry of longing many places in Scripture, none expresses this cry in more poignant words than King David at the death of his son. Picture this scene:

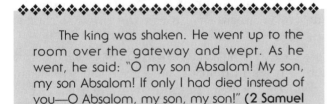

The king was shaken. He went up to the room over the gateway and wept. As he went, he said: "O my son Absalom! My son, my son Absalom! If only I had died instead of you—O Absalom, my son, my son!" **(2 Samuel 18:33)**

1. What thoughts might have filled David's cry of longing?

2. Session 2 ended by suggesting that you read **Romans 8:18–39**. Reread **verses 18–27** now.

I consider that our present sufferings are not worth comparing with the glory that will be revealed in us.

The creation waits in eager expectation for the sons of God to be revealed. For the creation was subjected to frustration, not by its own choice, but by the will of the one who subjected it, in hope that the creation itself will be liberated from its bondage to decay and brought into the glorious freedom of the children of God.

We know that the whole creation has been groaning as in the pains of childbirth right up to the present time. Not only so, but we ourselves, who have the firstfruits of the Spirit, groan inwardly as we wait eagerly for our adoption as sons, the redemption of our bodies.

For in this hope we were saved. But hope that is seen is no hope at all. Who hopes for what he already has? But if we hope for what we do not yet have, we wait for it patiently.

In the same way, the Spirit helps us in our weakness. We do not know what we ought to pray for, but the Spirit Himself intercedes for us with groans that words cannot express. And He who searches our hearts knows the mind of the Spirit, because the Spirit intercedes for the saints in accordance with God's will. (**Romans 8:18–27**)

a. Put brackets around the section of this passage that in your opinion expresses a cry of longing.

b. Who and what are longing?

c. When and how will this cry be hushed?

d. Someone has defined *hope* as "faith looking forward." Does this definition fit the way

25

❖

the apostle Paul uses the word *hope* in this passage? Explain.

Focusing on My Life

1. The cry of longing sometimes finds expression in "if only." Remember King David's lament over Absalom—"If only I had died instead of you"? Share with a partner one or two "if only's" you have felt during your own grief process.

2. The pain of longing can overwhelm us. The loneliness threatens to suffocate us. Tears well up again and again, and after we think we have cried all we can cry, we feel the tears begin to fall yet once more. Where can we find comfort during those times when our pain seems endless and we ourselves don't have a clue as to what might help us? Reread **Romans 8:26–27.**

a. Study those verses and **Romans 8:34.** In what specific way does each person of the Trinity help "us in our weakness," in those times when "we do not know what we ought to pray for"?

The Holy Spirit—

The Father—

The Lord Jesus—

b. How can this sure and certain knowledge kindle the warmth of hope in you, even when the cry of longing and the loneliness of grief chill your heart?

3. Someone has said of God, "Sometimes He calms the storm, sometimes He calms His child." Tell your partner about a time your Lord calmed you even while the storm of grief roared around you.

4. Believers down through the centuries have clung to God's promises in **Romans 8** during all kinds of storms. Read the final few verses of this chapter.

And we know that in all things God works for the good of those who love Him, who have been called according to His purpose.

For those God foreknew He also predestined to be conformed to the likeness of His Son, that He might be the firstborn among many brothers. And those He predestined, He also called; those He called, He also justified; those He justified, He also glorified.

What, then, shall we say in response to this? If God is for us, who can be against us? He who did not spare His own Son, but gave Him up for us all—how will He not also, along with Him, graciously give us all things?

Who will bring any charge against those whom God has chosen? It is God who justifies. Who is he that condemns? Christ Jesus, who died—more than that, who was raised to life—is at the right hand of God and is also interceding for us.

Who shall separate us from the love of Christ? Shall trouble or hardship or persecution or famine or nakedness or danger or sword? As it is written: "For Your sake we face death all day long; we are considered as sheep to be slaughtered."

No, in all these things we are more than conquerors through Him who loved us. For I am convinced that neither death nor life, neither angels nor demons, neither the present nor the future, nor any powers, neither height nor depth, nor anything else in all creation, will be able to separate us from the love of God that is in Christ Jesus our Lord. (**Romans 8:28–39**)

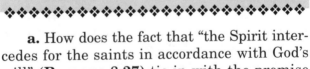

a. How does the fact that "the Spirit intercedes for the saints in accordance with God's will" **(Romans 8:27)** tie in with the promise that "in all things God works for the good of those who love Him, who have been called according to His purpose"?

b. Where in these verses from **Romans 8** do you most clearly see the cross?

c. How does the Gospel message—the truth that Jesus died and rose again to forgive you and to free you from death—guarantee that God will keep all the promises He makes in **Romans 8?**

d. Which verse(s) from **Romans 8** comforts you most when you think of your own cry of longing, especially the pain of loneliness?

Focusing on the Week Ahead

1. Read and meditate on **Psalm 42** and **Psalm 139.** Compare the feelings of the psalmist with your own.

2. Memorize your favorite verse(s) from **Romans 8.**

4

Grief: The Cry for Supportive Love

Focusing Our Sights

In this fourth session we will recognize the cry for supportive love in our grief. We will admit how lonely we can feel when others don't seem to understand. Finally, we will embrace God's freely-offered love extended to us through His Word and through His people, especially those who have walked the path of grief themselves.

Focusing Our Attention

How we needed love and support from others as we faced the reality of Becky's death. She died in Seattle, thousands of miles from our home in St. Louis. Questions flooded through our minds that day. What do we do next? How do we make funeral arrangements at a distance? If we fly home, how will we get our car back to Missouri? And the most important question of all: How do we go on from here?

God provided for our needs in abundance. We were overwhelmed by the care of so many Christian friends. I will never forget the chaplain's wordless bear hug. Or the calm compassion of a Christian nurse from India. Or the shared grief and practical help given by the pastor who had been our host in Seattle. Or the close friend who called the funeral home for us and who met us at the airport.

I will never forget the days at home before the funeral as the family gathered. We laughed and cried together. We read the Scriptures together. Our pastors helped us plan the funeral service.

I will never forget the young people who had known Becky and her fiancé Greg and who came to comfort us. Or Greg's brother and sister-in-law who volunteered to drive our car home. I will never forget the friends from work and church who came to comfort us, to bring food, to surround us with love at the funeral home and the church.

The support continued as I returned to work. As time passed, many were not sure what to say or ask. But Gail and I were deeply moved when someone sent an Easter lily two months later, when people sent cards of remembrance on Becky's birthday, when a friend phoned several months after the funeral to offer prayer support. We found ourselves moved again by the warm reception we received from students and faculty at Becky's former high school and church when we visited there after her death.

Even now, our need for support from other believers continues, but at a different level of intensity. We also now find ourselves motivated to reach out to others who need the support of others in their grieving.

Grief has the potential to bring out the best in the body of Christ. But it can also isolate and depress when no understanding ear is available.

❖

Think about a time you offered support to someone else during a time of grief in his or her life.

1. In light of your own recent grief experience, what kinds of comfort and support would you offer again?

2. What might you do differently? Why?

Focusing on the Issue

Mert and Irene Strommen write, "The cry for supportive love was more immediate. It arose out of the extreme sense of vulnerability we experienced over our son's sudden death. Emotionally we needed to be embraced in the arms of love, as a sobbing child needs to be held by a parent" (p. xii).

1. In what ways has your own cry for supportive love been like that of the Strommens'? How was it different?

2. What kind of support helped you the most at the time of your loved one's death?

Focusing on God's Word

Our Lord has placed us in relationships with others in His church. He intends that His sons and daughters comfort and support one another through the joys and the hard times of life. We experience His compassion and love for us as we receive it from our brothers and sisters in Christ. Read **2 Corinthians 1:3–7** for a description of how that happens.

❖❖❖❖❖❖❖❖❖❖❖❖❖❖❖❖❖❖❖❖❖❖❖❖

Praise be to the God and Father of our Lord Jesus Christ, the Father of compassion and the God of all comfort, who comforts us in all our troubles so that we can comfort those in any trouble, with the comfort we ourselves have received from God.

For just as the sufferings of Christ flow over into our lives, so also through Christ our comfort overflows. If we are distressed, it is for your comfort and salvation; if we are comforted, it is for your comfort, which produces in you patient endurance of the same sufferings we suffer. And our hope for you is firm, because we know that just as you share in our sufferings, so also you share in our comfort. (2 Corinthians 1:3–7)

❖❖❖❖❖❖❖❖❖❖❖❖❖❖❖❖❖❖❖❖❖❖❖❖

1. When Paul wrote these words of comfort, he had in mind the persecution he had been enduring as God's servant.

a. From the text, though, how can we tell that his words are God's word to us in any kind of trouble?

b. This passage describes at least four relationships. What are they?

c. What makes these relationships especially significant as we think about the consolation we need when we suffer in any way, but especially as we grieve life's losses?

2. Underline the word *all* each time it appears in the passage.

a. What makes this word significant when we find ourselves overwhelmed with the pain of suffering and grief?

b. What results does God's comfort produce in our lives? (Find them in the rest of the passage—there are at least three.)

3. Paul goes on to describe the extreme danger and hardship he has faced. Then he continues, "But this happened that we might not rely on ourselves but on God, who raises the dead. ... On Him we have set our hope that He will continue to deliver us, as you help us by your prayers" (**2 Corinthians 11:9–10**).

a. When might we be tempted to rely on ourselves while we grieve?

b. The "God of all comfort," the God who raises the dead has already delivered us from our fiercest enemies at the cross of Jesus Christ. What hope—sure and certain hope—does that give you as you think about the grief you're working through?

Focusing on My Life

1. How can you tell from the text you have just studied that it's not only okay to need the comfort and compassion of other believers in times of trouble, but that God Himself wants that for you?

2. What things make it hard for you to ask your brothers and sisters in Jesus for the kinds of support and love you need? What can you do to overcome that resistance?

3. What kinds of supportive love do you continue to need? How could you go about finding people willing to provide that?

Focusing on the Week Ahead

1. Let God use another believer to reach out to you in compassion with His comfort. Ask a brother or sister in the faith for a specific thing you need.

2. Let God use you to reach out to someone else in compassion with His comfort. This can involve a very simple action—perhaps you can pray for someone else who has experienced

❖

grief or loss. (Remember Paul's words—"He will continue to deliver us, *as you help us by your prayers*"). Or if you're ready to step out farther at this point in your journey, something that will involve more commitment, send a personal note of comfort, sit with someone who has suffered a very recent loss, take groceries or a meal to someone who grieves.

3. Read **Psalm 131** and **Psalm 143:1–8.** As you do, don't just read for information. Let the Holy Spirit speak His Word personally to your heart. What is He saying in these passages?

Grief: The Cry for Understanding

Focusing Our Sights

In this fifth session we will hear and explore the cry for understanding which raises the why questions about our loved one's death. We admit the ongoing search for answers and the feeling of anger toward others, ourselves, and God that often arise in the grieving process. We learn to redirect our anger toward sin and its consequences and entrust our questions to a loving God who sacrificed His own Son for us.

Focusing Our Attention

Why did Becky have to die? Only 23, she had so much going for her. She was a promising student of English and the humanities with a disciplined mind and a desire to teach young people. She had learned so many spiritual lessons during her illness and wanted to share her faith with others. She eagerly anticipated marriage to a fine young man and hoped for children.

We prayed for her healing. In fact, people across the country prayed for her. We supported her as best we could. She had the best doctors at the finest medical facility available. The extensive search for a bone marrow donor ended with the discovery of one perfect out of 600,000 entries in the nation-wide bone marrow registry. Becky had such inner strength, deep faith, and the will to live. Why did Becky have to die?

Throughout the process of accepting Becky's death and relying on God's promises, I have struggled to understand why she died. The cry goes on.

I remember attending a wedding one year to the day from Becky's engagement to Greg. The closing song at the wedding had also been the closing song at Becky's funeral. After the wedding reception, I went to our basement family room and paced the floor. I cried and cried with gut-wrenching sobs and fierce anger. Why? Why? Why?

Afterward, I felt a greater peace inside. And that weekend, Gail and I were able to share our feelings and needs with one another on a deeper level than before.

In session 1, we mentioned some of the myths that have grown up in some people's minds about grief and the process of grieving. One myth not on that original list might be stated like this: "Good Christians don't ask why questions." Do you agree that this idea is a myth? Explain.

❖

Focusing on the Issue

In *Five Cries of Grief,* the Strommens write, "The inevitable 'why' fuels our cry for understanding. It is the effort of our intellect to establish a bridge of understanding between our son's death and our acceptance of it, to attribute meaning to a meaningless loss" (p. xii).

1. Even though we can seldom construct a sturdy intellectual "bridge of understanding" where death and pain are concerned, human beings keep trying anyway.

a. Why do you think that is?

b. When might the attempt to understand why help us work through grief?

2. Under what conditions might the attempt "to attribute meaning to a meaningless loss" be less than helpful?

Focusing on God's Word

Some Christians have come to believe that all why questions are sinful. They think that it's somehow wrong to question God. Of course, sometimes this may be true. If our questions well up from hard, cold, bitter hearts, they cue us to look for deeper problems in our relationship with our Lord.

On the other hand, our Savior Himself asked His heavenly Father the why question from His cross **(Matthew 27:46)**. And in doing so, He quoted King David, the person whom God once called, "a man after My own heart" **(Psalm 22:1; Acts 13:22)**. From Job to Habakkuk the why question rings out from the pages of the Old Testament. Never does our Lord scold the one who asks it.

❖❖❖❖❖❖❖❖❖❖❖❖❖❖❖❖❖❖❖❖❖❖❖❖

My God, my God, why have You forsaken me? Why are You so far from saving me, so far from the words of my groaning? O my God, I cry out by day, but You do not answer, by night, and am not silent. Yet You are enthroned as the Holy One; You are the praise of Israel. In You our fathers put their trust; they trusted and You delivered them. They cried to You and were saved; in You they trusted and were not disappointed. (Psalm 22:1–5)

❖❖❖❖❖❖❖❖❖❖❖❖❖❖❖❖❖❖❖❖❖❖❖❖

1. Read **Psalm 22:1–5.**

a. What kind of an answer did the Lord give David in response to his questions in **verse 1?**

b. This instance is not unique. Almost always when God's people ask Him why, He replies in this same way. What do you conclude from this?

2. Now read **Psalm 131.** It's another psalm written by David.

❖❖❖❖❖❖❖❖❖❖❖❖❖❖❖❖❖❖❖❖❖❖❖❖❖❖

> My heart is not proud, O LORD, my eyes are not haughty; I do not concern myself with great matters or things too wonderful for me. But I have stilled and quieted my soul; like a weaned child with its mother, like a weaned child is my soul within me. O Israel, put your hope in the LORD both now and forevermore. (Psalm 131:1–3)

❖❖❖❖❖❖❖❖❖❖❖❖❖❖❖❖❖❖❖❖❖❖❖❖❖❖

a. With what answer to his why questions has David apparently found peace? Express his answer in your own words in the space below. Then talk about it with a partner.

b. Speculate a bit on how David got to **Psalm 131** from **Psalm 22.** What kind of process might have been involved?

3. In *Five Cries of Grief* Mert Strommen tells of a conversation he had with evangelist Leighton Ford. At the time of their conversation, each of these fathers had suffered the death of a son. Commenting on what Strommen later would call "the cry for understanding," Ford said, "I have come to realize that I understand God less, but trust Him more" (p. 76).

a. How does Ford's comment echo David's conclusion?

b. How satisfying do you find this conclusion at this stage of your own grief process? If you feel comfortable doing so explain your answer to your partner.

Focusing on My Life

1. Imagine your grieving process as a journey down a long and winding road. In relationship to the cry for understanding, how would you describe your current location? (*Check one and explain your choice to your partner.*)

_____ I took a short-cut around the why questions early in the trip and haven't been back to that place in the road since.

_____ I find myself going around and around the same loop again and again. I can't seem to get past it.

_____ I think I'm making steady progress, but then I find I'm back where I've started and I'm walking in circles.

_____ I've come back to that spot in the road several times, but each time I've gained new understanding.

_____ For now, at least, by God's grace I have seen enough of that scenery and am on my way past that stretch of the road.

_____ Other _____

2. Maybe you're asking the why questions in earnest right now.

a. If so, what do you think might help you as you wrestle through that process?

b. How has God's Word helped you in this struggle so far?

❖

c. What other things have you personally found helpful in this struggle that you could suggest to others?

Focusing on the Week Ahead

1. Plan at least one way to get the help you thought about as you answered question 2a above. Then, relying on God's grace, follow your plan.

2. Meditate on **Revelation 21:1–4** or **Hebrews 12:1–3.** Memorize some or all of these passages if you can.

❖

Grief: The Cry for Significance

Focusing Our Sights

In this final session we utter the cry for significance. Even as we find ultimate significance in the life, death, and resurrection of Jesus Christ for our salvation, we recognize our need to see something good come out of seeming tragedy. We learn to direct our grieving into constructive channels of living for others and bearing witness to God's faithfulness to us in our grieving process.

Focusing Our Attention

As I flew over Montana enroute to St. Louis from Seattle on the morning after Becky's death, I wrote these words in my journal:

"We are filled with emotion—not much sleep last night after busy packing, many tears, mutual hugs—but we rejoice for Becky and see God's plan for her and for us through the tears—God's plans, not to harm but to prosper, plans for hope and a future (Jeremiah 29:11).

"I want to help two things happen—some type of ongoing memorial funding at both Concordia Lutheran High School in Fort Wayne and at Valparaiso University in Becky's honor

and some way of telling Becky's story and the impact of her life and illness on the lives of many people and many churches who prayed for us and supported us."

That cry for significance has led to some meaningful actions and events. A scholarship fund in Becky's memory provides yearly scholarships for students at Concordia High School in Fort Wayne. I have had opportunity to address the student body to express our thanks and to present some of the scholarships personally. Valparaiso University has created an annual award for a female scholar-athlete in Becky's memory, and again the family was present for the initial award. A special banner was also commissioned as a memorial for Concordia University, River Forest, Illinois, where Becky also attended. Congregations to which our family belonged at one time in both Fort Wayne and Peru, Indiana, have also memorialized Becky. This Bible study on grief has given us the opportunity to tell Becky's story.

I thank God for His faithfulness in Becky's life and in our lives since her death. Our Lord has given significance to our loss.

1. How does the cry for understanding differ from the cry for significance?

2. Think about this cry for significance.

a. Have you experienced it? If so, tell a little about how and when it began.

❖

b. If not, can you see any clues in your grief process that indicates this cry might be your own sometime in the days and weeks ahead?

Focusing on the Issue

Mert Strommen describes his personal cry for significance at the death of his son in these words:

❖❖❖❖❖❖❖❖❖❖❖❖❖❖❖❖❖❖❖❖❖❖❖❖❖❖❖

With death, facts become unalterable. Yet within me continues to well up a cry that Dave's shortened life be continued in some way, that his decision to serve, gained after struggle and prayer, not be buried. At his death, I felt keenly the need to see something develop that would be an extension of his ministry, that would bring meaning to a positive life wasted by death. Since then I have come to realize how universal the cry is (p. 94).

❖❖❖❖❖❖❖❖❖❖❖❖❖❖❖❖❖❖❖❖❖❖❖❖❖❖❖

1. Do you agree with Strommen that this cry is universal? Explain your thoughts and opinions to your partner.

2. Note Strommen's exact words: "I felt keenly the need to see something develop that would bring meaning to a positive *life*" (emphasis added).

a. When might the cry for significance lead survivors to memorialize the *life* of their loved one?

b. When might the cry for significance lead survivors to memorialize the *death* of their loved one?

.

3. How well does the custom of designating memorials after someone has died help still the cry for significance? Explain.

4. What examples can you name in which survivors found ways to bring significance to their loved ones' life? death?

❖

Focusing on God's Word

In **Hebrews 11,** the Holy Spirit recounts thumbnail sketches of the lives and, in some cases, the deaths of His faithful servants from Old Testament history. These men and women form the "great cloud of witnesses" mentioned in **verse 1** of the next chapter of **Hebrews.** Read **Hebrews 12:1–3.**

❖❖❖❖❖❖❖❖❖❖❖❖❖❖❖❖❖❖❖❖❖❖❖❖❖❖

Therefore, since we are surrounded by such a great cloud of witnesses, let us throw off everything that hinders and the sin that so easily entangles, and let us run with perseverance the race marked out for us. Let us fix our eyes on Jesus, the author and perfecter of our faith, who for the joy set before Him endured the cross, scorning its shame, and sat down at the right hand of the throne of God. Consider Him who endured such opposition from sinful men, so that you will not grow weary and lose heart. (Hebrews 12:1–3)

❖❖❖❖❖❖❖❖❖❖❖❖❖❖❖❖❖❖❖❖❖❖❖❖❖❖

1. In one sense, Abraham, Sarah, Rahab, Samson, and the rest of the "witnesses" listed in **Hebrews 11** all died prematurely. Why? Because when they died "none of them [had yet] received what had been promised." The world's Savior whom God had promised to send had not yet come.

a. In what ways are the lives of these witnesses an ongoing memorial to our Lord? (See **Hebrews 11** for more information.)

b. Nevertheless, the writer of **Hebrews** points us to Jesus and to the cross rather than to the saints who have gone before us. Why would that be?

2. How can "consider[ing] Him" keep us safe from the temptation to "grow weary and lose heart," even as we grieve the loss of those we love? Talk about this with a partner.

Focusing on My Life

1. When might it be sinful, even idolatrous, to memorialize a loved one who has died?

2. How can memorializing a loved one be a true act of worship?

3. As you think about the significance of your loved one's life and/or death, what kind of memorial could be fitting? (Feel free to think about traditional memorials like flowers at the grave site and monetary donations, but also think beyond them to things like the way you live your own personal life, the witness you want to give, the traits of your loved one you would like to exhibit in your own life and pass on to others, and so on.) Dream together with your partner about your ideas.

4. Which of your ideas have you already begun to implement? How?

5. Did you come up with any new insights about a memorial you would like to implement? If so, what step might you take today to set plans for that memorial in motion?

❖

Focusing on the Week Ahead

1. Continue to plan ways to answer the cry for significance that wells up from the life and death of your loved one. Talk about those plans with at least one other person. Notice how this process affects your feelings.

2. Meditate on **Genesis 50,** particularly on **verses 15–21.** What kinds of memorials did Joseph erect (in several senses) to his father, Jacob? What significance do you see in Joseph's actions for your own grief?

3. Memorize **Jeremiah 29:11.**

Notes for the Leader

1
Grief: Facing Your Loss

❖ Getting Ready

Arrive early—before anyone else will. Check the setting:
Is the room at a comfortable temperature?
Are the chairs arranged so that everyone will be able to see everyone else without straining or turning around?
Is the lighting adequate?
Do you have some kind of soft drinks, tea, or coffee available? (This will help most people feel more at ease.)
Do you have plenty of tissues and is the box readily accessible without being conspicuous?
Do you have name tags and marking pens (if you will need them)?
Do you have Bibles for those who do not bring their own?

Then, before the group arrives, spend some time in prayer. Ask the Lord who truly is the "God of all comfort" **(2 Corinthians 1:3),** to guide both you and each group member as you talk, share, and support one another. Ask that God will help group members to be appropriately open with each other and that through His Word, He will console and strengthen each of you as you walk together down the road of grief.

❖ Getting Started

(*About 5 Minutes.*) Welcome each participant warmly and introduce yourself as necessary. Make sure all participants know one another, too. If even one person does not know the others very well, provide name tags for everyone, at least for the first few times you get together.

Briefly explain the purpose of the group—to provide mutual comfort and support in Christ while you each walk your individual paths of grief. Remind the group that no one grieves in exactly the same way. Explain that most of the time you will listen to each other and share God's comfort in Jesus.

Gently but firmly make it clear that you're not here to "fix" each other, to advise one another, or to provide psychological counsel or therapy. Rather, you will gather each time around God's Word, anticipating and expecting Him to use His Word to strengthen and guide you.

You may also want to point out that these materials will focus primarily on the person in grief and on the process of grief. The materials are designed to clarify the grief process and to help make it less unfamiliar and frightening. The process itself will no doubt still hurt and for many it will prove turbulent. (Other courses offered by CPH focus primarily on God's promises of eternal life for His children and on the sure and certain hope of the resurrection [e.g., *Walking in the Shadows,* order no. 20-2380 (study guide) and 20-2381 (leaders guide)].

Note: As you lead this course, keep in mind the possibility that one or more group members may be mourning the death of someone who did not have a living relationship with Christ or someone whose eternal salvation remains a question. Until you *know for sure,* avoid trying to comfort the group with blanket statements like "We can rejoice that we will be reunited with our loved ones in heaven." Rather, focus your attention on the grievers themselves and on the comfort God has promised us as we, by His grace, discover ways to live with death, to do our grief work.

❖ Focusing Our Sights

(*About 1 Minute.*) This heading signals the goal statement for each session of this course. Research in adult education indicates that when people have a clear idea about where a leader intends to go, they are much more likely to arrive at that point with the leader as the session ends. Read the goal statement to the group.

❖ Focusing Our Attention

(*About 7 Minutes.*) Read the story about Becky. Note that it is the first installment of a narrative that will run through all six sessions of this course. It tells part of the story of the author's own grief.

1. When the narrative ends, ask participants to form groups of two. Ask that they not choose a close family member. Allow about a minute for each person to comment on Becky's story, two minutes total.

2. Again ask participants to work with a partner to make their lists. Allow about two minutes for this, then share lists with the whole group. The point here is that any death touches numbers of people in many significant ways. Grief is not a "little thing," but a significant challenge all of us face while we live here on this earth.

❖ Focusing on the Issue

(*About 10 Minutes.*) Read or summarize the material that introduces this part of the study. Focus especially on the myths about grief.

1. Pose these two questions to the group one at a time.

2. This question gives participants a chance to personalize your discussion in number 1. Ask that they talk with their partners about it. Allow about four minutes for this discussion.

3. Now call for everyone's attention and discuss why each myth, while perhaps sounding fine on first reading, is in fact untrue and harmful. Let the participants point out the flaws in the myths as much as possible, but add your own comments as necessary.

If no one mentions it, do point out that each myth begins with the phrase "if your faith is strong enough." This phrase in and of itself should raise our suspicions because it focuses us on our own faith as the source of our strength rather than pointing us to the words and promises of our Lord.

In addition, each of the myths in its own way denigrates the emotions our Creator has given us as His good gifts to us. He Himself experiences each of the emotions named here. The ability to experience emotions are one way He has made us like Himself. Don't dwell too long on these points; you will encounter these truths again as you explore today's Scripture reading.

❖ Focusing on God's Word

(*About 12 Minutes.*) Because of its length, this Scripture reading has not been reproduced in the guide. Make sure everyone has a Bible as you begin. Ask volunteers to take turns reading **John 11.** The narrative will probably be a familiar one to most participants, so it may not be necessary for you to spend much time explaining the events or their sequence. Do, however, note that the incident took place on the Saturday before Palm Sunday, less than a week before the crucifixion.

To break up the reading, you might assign parts—a narrator, Jesus, the disciples, Mary, and Martha. Read the account directly from the Bible.

1. Ask the group to work together to identify these responses. For instance, in **v. 21** some participants may note trust and perhaps frustration or even anger. In **vv. 24** and **27,** we hear Martha express her faith and the peace that God's promises have given her. In **v. 33** we see deep sorrow in those who had come to mourn with the family and in Mary herself. This is mirrored in Christ Himself in **v. 35.** In **v. 37,** we see skepticism or perhaps many "why, Lord?" questions. Accept other reasonable responses.

58
❖

2. Jesus did not scold anyone. He understood the process of grief and continued to love the mourners, even when they felt their emotions to the depths, even when they seemed to question His compassion. He grieved with them.

3. This question may draw a variety of responses. Because Christ loved them, He came to them. He comforted them with His promises and His presence. And He reunited them—temporarily. Lazarus would die again; Mary and Martha would also die someday; Jesus Himself faced His own death which would come very soon. But even as He proved His power over death by raising Lazarus, He would magnify this victory by rising to life Himself on Easter. In this victory, He proved Himself both willing and able to help and comfort us in every time of need and to bring us safely through every shadowy valley through which we must walk in this life.

❖ Focusing on My Life

(*About 25 Minutes.*) **1.** Introduce this activity by reading the directions to the group. Encourage them to follow the guidelines suggested in the study guide. Emphasize especially the directions for the listeners. Tell the participants they will each have five minutes to tell their story to their partner; then the listeners will become speakers and vice versa. Signal the groups when one minute remains. Then call time after five minutes.

2. Call for the group's attention when time has elapsed. Then read this question to them. Ask that they again work with their partner to answer the questions here, taking turns. Allow about six minutes each for the partners to share. Encourage the listeners to simply listen and thereby support the partner who is speaking. Again, give a "one-minute warning" and call time at the end of six minutes.

3. This final exercise gives participants a chance to connect their faith with their feelings and to pray for one another. Read the directions to the group and ask that they follow them. If some would like to pray together quietly in class now, encourage that. If some do not feel comfortable in doing so, urge them to jot some notes so they will remember what to ask of God when they pray on their own during the coming week.

❖ Focusing on the Week Ahead

(*About 2 Minutes.*) Urge participants to complete one or more of the activities. Encourage everyone to do activity 1; suggest that some may want to do activity 2 also.

❖ To Close

(*About 1 Minute.*) Speak **Hebrews 13:20–21** as a blessing before you dismiss the group:

May the God of peace, who through the blood of the eternal covenant brought back from the dead our Lord Jesus, that great Shepherd of the sheep, equip you with everything good for doing His will, and may He work in us what is pleasing to Him, through Jesus Christ, to whom be glory for ever and ever. Amen.

2
Grief: The Cry of Pain

❖ Focusing Our Sights

(*About 3 Minutes.*) Welcome everyone warmly. Provide name tags again if it's necessary in your situation. Read aloud the focus statement.

❖ Focusing Our Attention

(*About 7 Minutes.*) Read the next installment of Becky's story aloud. The two questions that follow will serve as an introduction to today's topic. Talk about them in the whole group, giving individuals the opportunity to share. Do not force anyone to do so, however.

❖ Focusing on the Issue

(*About 10 Minutes.*) This material sets up the organizing thoughts around which the rest of this course will revolve. Summarize the ideas, perhaps writing the "five cries" on chart paper or a chalkboard. After a brief summary, ask if anyone would like any point clarified. Don't stop too long to discuss the individual "cries" right now. Instead, tell the group that today and during each of the four sessions after this one you will focus on one of these "cries," exploring it in depth.

1. Ask the group to comment on this. Accept volunteers' responses.

2. Again, ask the group to comment. Accept reasonable responses.

3. Talk about this together, too.

❖ Focusing on God's Word

(*About 10 Minutes.*) Read aloud or invite volunteers to read **Lamentations 3:16–33.**

Before the reading, note that the book of Lamentations is an extended poem expressing the pain of the prophet Jeremiah at seeing his nation invaded by an army. Thousands died horrible deaths at the hands of the invaders, countless others were marched off into captivity by an enemy that showed little mercy. No doubt, the prophet personally witnessed many individual tragedies in addition to the overall disaster.

After the initial reading, ask participants to go back over the reading and mark the text with brackets as suggested in question 1 and underline the words suggested in question 2.

1. Most participants will probably bracket part or all of the first two paragraphs.

2. Most participants will probably underline part or all of the last three paragraphs.

3. Talk together about this question. Lead the group to see that while God strengthens His people and supports us *in* our grief, He never short-circuits the process for dealing with loss. Trauma, loss, tragedy—all of these pain God's heart, and they pain the hearts of His children, too. God grieves our losses with us, and as we saw last time, He never rebukes us for our grief.

❖ Focusing on My Life

(*About 25 Minutes.*) The next set of questions is intended for discussion between two participants. You know your group. Decide whether or not it would be best for everyone to choose a different partner than the person they paired up with last time or if it would be best to repeat the pairs from last time. If you have no strong leanings, you may want to leave it up to the group.

As the group moves through the questions that follow, announce the time limitations for each and serve as timer for the group. Walk around and listen in unobtrusively, but don't offer comments unless someone invites you to.

1. Allow about two minutes for this question.

2. Allow about three minutes for this question.

3. Allow about 10 minutes for this set of questions.

4. Allow about 10 minutes for this set of questions.

As the discussion for question number 4 winds down, call for the group's attention. Ask volunteers to summarize particularly helpful insights or ideas they talked about with their partners. If no one else does so, refer back to question **4b**. As we look to the cross, we remember that God gave up His only

Son into death for our sins. Since He has not withheld His own dearly loved Son but delivered Jesus into death for our sakes, we can be certain He will keep all His other many promises to us as well.

❖ Focusing on the Week Ahead

(*About 2 Minutes.*) Point out the activities listed here. Encourage everyone to do the first one; suggest that some may want to do the second also.

❖ To Close

(*About 5 Minutes.*) Read either **Lamentations 3:16–33** or **Psalm 73:21–26** as a closing prayer of praise and an affirmation of trust in the God who has promised never to fail us or forsake us.

3
Grief: The Cry of Longing

❖ Focusing Our Sights

(*About 5 Minutes.*) Warmly welcome each participant. Provide name tags if they are needed. Then read today's goal statement.

❖ Focusing Our Attention

(*About 5 Minutes.*) Remind the group that sessions 2–6

follow the organizing principle introduced last time—what Mert and Irene Strommen have called the "five cries of grief." Today you will focus together on the "cry of longing." Encourage the group to read the next excerpt from Becky's story with an eye toward seeing if participants can discover some of the facets that might be involved in this "cry of longing." Then read the story to the group yourself.

Talk briefly about the "cry of longing." How would group members describe it to a friend who has, perhaps, not yet experienced a time of deep personal grief? Accept reasonable answers, and then move right into the next section which clarifies the concept further.

❖ Focusing on the Issue

(*About 15 Minutes.*) Read or summarize the first two paragraphs. Then tell the group that the three questions that follow are designed for partner-pairs to share. Keep time for the groups, allowing each person about two minutes to respond to each question. Again today, encourage each person to take a turn speaking and then listening.

Urge listeners to simply listen in an accepting way. This is not the time to give advice or to solve anyone else's problems. While it may not seem so, the simple act of listening to someone else's hurts and expressing concern for that person's pain is much more helpful than any attempts to "fix" their grief.

❖ Focusing on God's Word

(*About 12 Minutes.*) Introduce this part of the session by reading David's lament for Absalom. You might ask if anyone remembers the circumstances of this young man's death and why those circumstances made it much more tragic.

Absalom was killed while leading an insurrection against his father, David. David had made a series of mistakes stretching over a period of years, despite the deep love he had for Absalom. After awhile, Absalom's heart grew harder and colder toward David until finally his rebellion grew—literally—into treason. The two did not have a chance to reconcile before Absalom died.

1. Let the group speculate on this. Probably most responses will involve thoughts beginning with "if only."

2. You might suggest that the group read this passage aloud in unison. Then work together on the four questions that follow.

a. Let individuals do this, then ask volunteers to comment. Many will probably bracket phrases in the second or third paragraphs. Accept reasonable responses. You may want to read these verses from a contemporary paraphrase (e.g., The Living Bible) if some in the group have trouble understanding the apostle's line of reasoning here.

b. We (God's people) long for our full salvation to be revealed when Jesus comes again. The creation itself also longs for that day. (See paragraph 3.)

c. The text refers to the time as the time of "our adoption as sons" and "the redemption of our bodies." These are both references to the day when God's work in us reaches full completion—Judgment Day.

d. Explain that when the Bible uses the word *hope*, it means something sure and certain. We sometimes use the term as a synonym for the thought "I wish it could be." But biblical hope *never* disappoints us. Let participants comment on the way Paul uses *hope* here.

❖ Focusing on My Life

(*About 20 Minutes.*) **1.** Have each individual work together with a partner to respond to this question. Allow about one minute each for this sharing.

2. Encourage partners to work together on this question, too.

a. Note that **Romans 8:34** is found later in this session

in the study guide. It clearly states that our Lord Jesus intercedes for us. **Romans 8:26–27** points us to the Holy Spirit's
intercession on our behalf. So the Father hears the intercession of both the Son and the Spirit. Together, all three per-
sons of the Trinity are working to help us in our times of
weakness. Allow two minutes or so for this discussion.

b. Let participants discuss this with a partner. Allow
about four minutes total.

3. Allow about three minutes each for this discussion, six
minutes total.

4. At this point tell the group they have about six minutes left. Ask that everyone respond to **d** and then use the
remaining time to work through any of the other three questions they would like to discuss with their partners.

❖ Focusing on the Week Ahead

(*About 2 Minutes.*) Call participants' attention again to
the activities. Encourage everyone to do the first one; suggest
that some may want to do the second also.

❖ To Close

(*About 5 Minutes.*) If participants take their study guides
home, encourage them to look back over today's lesson several
times during this week. Which passages touch them in a particularly meaningful, faith-strengthening way? Have them
share some of their favorite passages as a closing.

4
Grief: The Cry
for Supportive Love

❖ Focusing Our Sights

(*About 2 Minutes.*) Read today's goal statement and briefly remind the group that today you will deal with the third of the "five cries of grief"—the "cry for supportive love."

❖ Focusing Our Attention

(*About 8 Minutes.*) Move into today's part of the ongoing story about Becky's death and its aftermath in the lives of her family members. When you have finished this reading, work with the group to answer the two questions that follow. Both call for opinions and personal observations. Accept insights volunteers offer.

❖ Focusing on the Issue

(*About 10 Minutes.*) Again today, read or summarize the paragraph that introduces this part of the study. Before individuals answer the questions here, note that because of the circumstances surrounding Becky's family and the Strommens and their family, both groups seem to have received lots of loving support from friends, church, and co-workers. The experience of the people in the group may resemble this or it may differ quite markedly from it.

Ask that the participants choose partners with whom they can work comfortably. They are to answer the two questions that follow in this part of the lesson. Allow about two minutes each for sharing.

1–2. If some have not received all the help they needed, ask that they keep these needs in reserve; we will discuss them later. For now, they should focus on the support they have received as they answer the questions. Again, allow about two minutes each for sharing responses to each question.

❖ Focusing on God's Word

(*About 15 Minutes.*) **1.** Read **2 Corinthians 1:3–7** to the group. Then work together through the study material that follows.

a. Probably someone will point to the phrase "who comforts us in *all* our troubles."

b. The four relationships include the relationship between the Father and Jesus, between us and the Father, between us and Jesus, and between us and other believers.

c. Let participants talk this over with a partner and then share with the whole group. Probably most will conclude that suffering loss, grief, pain, and other kinds of trouble is in and of itself bad enough. When we suffer alone, the trouble is magnified many times over. To know that we have a relationship with the heavenly Father through Jesus Christ, to know (as we saw last time) that Jesus intercedes for us, to know that our brothers and sisters in the faith want to comfort us and encourage us as we move through the process of grieving—this knowledge is a precious, a priceless treasure.

2. After individuals have underlined the word *all*, have them discuss the questions.

a. Accept responses from volunteers. Most will probably note that no matter how big our pain, God's consolation will be even bigger.

b. God's comfort produces patient endurance, hope for the future, and the capacity to comfort others.

3. Read the paragraph here that sets up the questions that follow.

a. Accept reasonable responses from the group. Then give individuals a chance to talk with their partners about the times when they are most likely to try to rely on themselves rather than setting their hope in God.

b. Let participants discuss this, too, with their partners. It's not a new idea—we've run into it several times as we've worked through this course. God kept His promise to send Jesus to die for us; since He's already given us His very best gift, we can trust Him to provide everything else we need.

❖ Focusing on My Life

(*About 10 Minutes.*) **1.** Accept reasonable responses. Paul's description assumes God's people will love, care for, and comfort one another as they encounter the trials of this life. In this way, they will demonstrate Christ's love to one another.

2. We mentioned before that not everyone who grieves receives the kind of supportive love all of us need from one another in the body of Christ. The idea here is not to find fault, but rather to find solutions. Let the group discuss the things that stand in their way of asking for the specific love and support they need. Sometimes with our fellow human beings, as with the Lord, we "do not have, because [we] do not ask" (**James 4:2**).

After the group members have had time to discuss this, call the whole group back together. Remind them of the support you are able to give one another in this group. Also remind each other that this is a gift from God through His people—the other group members.

Remind one another of the support available in your congregation through the regular worship services in which Christ ministers to each of you through His Word. If it's not likely to hurt someone in the group who is struggling through the process of grieving for a loved one who died outside the

Christian faith, point out that as Christians, we experience a great continuity between this life and the life hereafter. We understand the communion of saints to exist across the boundaries of both space and time. We can and do desperately miss the physical presence of our loved one, but we can also believe that we will be reunited at the heavenly throne of Christ, the Lamb of God.

3. This question is intended to move participants to an even more concrete discussion with their partners regarding their needs right now. Encourage them to be specific in stating these needs (e.g., someone to sit with them in church, a hug, someone to change the oil in the lawn mower, someone to call them once a day to see how they're doing). Encourage partners to brainstorm the who, the what, the where, and the how of each response they jot down.

❖ Focusing on the Week Ahead

(*About 5 Minutes.*) Read the suggested activities to the group. Then offer a prayer for each group member yourself. Ask that God would help each one find the courage and compassion he or she needs to receive His care from others and to extend that care to others.

1. The brainstorming that ends this session needs to "find feet." Accordingly, this assignment asks each participant to choose at least one item from the list of needs they just made and ask for help with that specific thing. Encourage them to do this, even if it feels awkward. Also encourage them to determine ahead of time to ask someone else if the first person they ask cannot help for one reason or another. Ask each partner-pair to chat briefly toward the end of the week, checking to see how the other person has followed through.

2. We need to lower our barriers and receive love from our Christian brothers and sisters. We also need to give that love and comfort. Here again, the journey can begin with one small step. Encourage partners to check on each other concerning this assignment when they chat later in the week.

❖ To Close

(*About 5 Minutes.*) Read aloud **Psalm 131** and/or **Psalm 143:1–8.**

5
Grief: The Cry
for Understanding

❖ Focusing Our Sights

(*About 3 Minutes.*) As you begin again today read the goal statement. Briefly review the previous three cries of grief— the cry of pain, the cry of longing, and the cry for supportive love. Tell the group as you did in session 2 that rather than being consecutive, air-tight stages, these descriptions of the grief process can recycle several times. Any given cry may last for a shorter or longer span of time.

Then, too, every individual's grieving process will differ and it will be different for each separate loss. We need not second guess ourselves. Trying to cut the process short will hurt, not help us. We can give ourselves permission to grieve when we realize that our Lord understands and stands by us in our grief.

Remembering these things is important as we begin this particular study. For some people, the why questions last only a few moments or days. Others, just as faithful to their Lord and just as spiritually mature struggle with the issues raised in this session for months or perhaps even longer. The Lord does not condemn our questions. We need not condemn ourselves for asking them.

❖ Focusing Our Attention

(*About 7 Minutes.*) Read the account describing part of the struggle Becky's father experienced with the cry for understanding. Then ask the group to comment on the myth that "good Christians don't ask why questions." Let individuals express their opinions, but ask that they explain the reasoning behind those opinions. You will look at some pertinent biblical data later, so don't spend too much time on these questions now.

❖ Focusing on the Issue

(*About 7 Minutes.*) The first paragraph here describes the "cry for understanding" in poignant terms. Read it aloud and then poll the group to see how many individuals have already asked some why questions of their own.

1. Let the group speculate as to the reason we can seldom construct a "bridge of understanding," but we keep trying. Then discuss the questions that follow.

a. Again, it's probably good to point out that such questioning isn't in and of itself necessarily wrong. God has created each of us—intellect and all. Human beings are "meaning makers"; most of us realize instinctively that we live in an orderly, rational universe created by a God of order. When we see apparent chaos, we try to make sense of it.

b. Such a struggle may throw us back to God, to His Word, and to the cross of Jesus Christ. Then our restless urge to understand comes under the sanctifying hand of the Holy Spirit and works a stronger, more mature and settled faith in us.

2. Like any circumstance of life, the seemingly chaotic events that pull our loved ones away from us in death and our attempts to understand the meaning of apparently meaningless loss can draw us away from God if we let our hearts become hard, cold, and bitter. If we refuse to let God work in us through His means of grace, we cut ourselves off from our only source of strength and from the only true solution in our search for meaning.

❖ Focusing on God's Word

(*About 25 Minutes.*) The two paragraphs that begin this section summarize the conversation so far. Ask a volunteer to read each. Before you go on, ask if anyone is surprised to find so much questioning going on in the Scripture and so little of it drawing one word of reprimand from our Lord. You may wish to point out that many Bible scholars believe Job to be the oldest Bible book while Habakkuk was written only 600 years or so before Jesus' birth. We might say the questioning went on practically from beginning to end among the Old Testament prophets.

1. Have someone read the first five verses of **Psalm 22** aloud for the group.

a. We see from **verses 3–5** that the Holy Spirit did not answer David's why questions directly. Instead, from the words David wrote next, we can deduce that the Spirit must have reminded David of His goodness to His people in the past. David reflected on that and found courage to believe that the Lord who had provided so much grace would not fail to do so now in David's present emergency or time of need.

b. Let participants comment. If no one mentions it, conclude this part of the discussion by observing that quite often the Lord Himself—His presence, love, and mercy—is the "answer" we really need when we find ourselves in distress. Rather than giving us an intellectual explanation (which we probably could not understand), our Lord frequently gives us Himself. Jesus comes to each of us personally through Word and sacrament to calm our fears and soothe our anguish.

2. Now have a volunteer read **Psalm 131** or ask the whole group to do so aloud.

a. Invite individuals to answer the question for themselves and then discuss it with a partner.

b. Point out that the same author who penned the

anguished cries of **Psalm 22:1–2** also wrote the words of calm trust recorded in **Psalm 131.** The Holy Spirit had apparently calmed His child's heart as He walked close to him as David continued to ask his questions and meditate on God's Word.

It would probably be worth noting for the group again that in some cases this part of the grieving process may take no longer than five minutes, while for other believers the questions may linger much longer. In either case, we will not be damaged by our questions if we let them drive us to our Savior's arms for comfort and consolation. He not only *has* the answers we seek, He Himself *is* the answer we need.

3. Let participants discuss with their partners this paragraph and the two questions that follow.

❖ Focusing on My Life

(*About 10 Minutes.*) **1.** Give participants time to read and respond to the exercise here. Then ask them to explain to their partners the statement they checked and their reasons for choosing.

2. Give participants a few minutes to jot down answers to the questions. Then ask volunteers to comment on **b** and **c.** Encourage individuals to take steps to get the kind of help they mentioned in **a.**

❖ Focusing on the Week Ahead

(*About 1 Minutes.*) Note the suggested activities. Encourage participants to complete them.

❖ To Close

(*About 5 Minutes.*) Read **Psalm 22:1–5.** Then invite a vol-

74

unteer to read aloud **Psalm 23.** Comment that we probably are not surprised that **Psalm 23** follows **Psalm 22.**

Psalm 22 goes on, after the verses we read today, to prophesy about the Shepherd who would lay down His life for the sheep. It is not an accident that it's followed by **Psalm 23,** the psalm that so many of God's people treasure for the peaceful picture it paints of Jesus, the Good Shepherd who cares for us even when we walk through "the valley of the shadow of death."

Psalm 22, as we saw today, raises the anguished question "Why, God?" It is not just by accident that these words come right before the psalm that most powerfully expresses the tender love of the Good Shepherd who is Himself the answer to our fevered questions.

Read (or recite from memory) **Psalm 23** together as you close.

6
Grief: The Cry for Significance

❖ Focusing Our Sights

(*About 3 Minutes.*) Welcome each participant warmly to your last session and review the first four "cries of grief"—the cry of pain, the cry of longing, the cry for supportive love, and the cry for understanding. Simply mentioning them and asking if anyone has any questions about any of them will probably be sufficient. Then read today's goal statement.

❖ Focusing Our Attention

(*About 5 Minutes.*) Read the last installment of Becky's story.

1. Ask volunteers from the group to comment. Look for remarks that indicate that "the cry for understanding" most often becomes a why question, while "the cry for significance" is more a "now what" or "how can my loved one's life/death have meaning?"

2. Ask participants to talk about questions **a** and **b** with a partner. You need not gather comments from the group before you move on into the next section of the lesson; simply let the group talk one-on-one for 3–5 minutes.

❖ Focusing on the Issue

(*About 8 Minutes.*) **1.** Have a volunteer read Mert Strommen's comments aloud to the group or read them yourself. Then ask participants to discuss this question with a partner. After a few moments, poll volunteers in the group for their opinions and for the evidence they considered in arriving at their conclusions. Simply accept what they say; there are no right or wrong answers.

2. Again, read Strommen's comments and then ask group members to talk about questions **a** and **b** with their partner. Note that survivors quite often memorialize *both* the life and the death of their loved one. Again, there are no right or wrong answers. If some participants need help, ask volunteers from the group to mention examples they have experienced or know about.

3. This is another opinion question designed to stimulate the kind of foundational thinking that needs to happen before the activities in "Focusing on My Life." Give the group time to discuss this now, either together or with partners.

4. Answers here may or may not be similar to those from number 2 above. Mothers Against Drunk Driving (MADD), for example, was started by a mother who grieved the death of her child due to a drunk driver. The group will probably know of other examples.

❖ Focusing on God's Word

(*About 10 Minutes.*) Read the section's opening paragraphs to the group. Clarify any facts as necessary. You may want to ask participants to find **Hebrews 11–12** in their own Bibles.

1. a. As we study and meditate on the lives of God's Old Testament people of faith, we see God's faithfulness to them. The Holy Spirit strengthens our faith in the truth that our Lord will prove Himself every bit as faithful to us in our times of need. We are encouraged as we see how God protected them and gave them a share in the work of bringing His kingdom and His reconciliation to sinful humanity.

b. Our Lord Jesus, through His cross and open tomb, made the victory of God's Old Testament saints possible. That same Lord makes our victory possible, too. We praise God for working in the lives of those who have gone to heaven before us and we honor both Him and those we love who have died in faith by using His strength and forgiveness to live in the confidence He wants us to enjoy.

2. Let partners talk about this. The text includes many encouraging phrases. When you call for the group's attention, ask if any volunteers would like to share a particular insight aloud.

❖ Focusing on My Life

(*About 20 Minutes.*) **1.** We have included this question and the next as a kind of safeguard against the lack of balance that could develop as a result of Satan's temptations to focus on the gifts of God (in this case, our loved ones) rather than on the Giver Himself. God's people know that beauty of spirit, kindness of heart, commitment of life, and faith in the

77
❖

Savior all come *from Him* as He works in us through His Word and the sacraments. These are not attributes we build up in ourselves. This is true also for our loved ones, and if they could speak to us from the glories of heaven, they would certainly testify to this fact. Even those who die outside the faith can perform worldly acts of kindness and love only because of the power they receive from our Lord. Accordingly, the honor and glory for the accomplishments of anyone's life rightly belong *only* to Him.

2. When we acknowledge the Lord as the source of all good in the lives of our loved ones our memorializing is an act of worship to God.

3. Ask individual participants to think about this on their own and to jot down the ideas that come to their minds. After five minutes or so, call for the group's attention and ask that they now discuss their ideas with their partner. Encourage listeners to be supportive. This is a brainstorming session of sorts. All ideas—no matter how impractical or seemingly silly—belong on the table at this point. Encourage everyone to dream a little.

4. This question won't require much discussion or prior thought. Simply have partners share their answers with each other.

5. Tell participants they can have a few minutes of time for personal thought and planning. Encourage them to jot down some of their ideas and plans in the space provided. Urge them to pray about their plans as they write.

Focusing on the Week Ahead

(*About 2 Minutes.*) Call participants' attention to the suggested activities. Urge participants to complete one or more.

To Close

(*About 10 Minutes.*) Because this is your last session,

allow a few extra minutes for today's closing. Point out that any loss brings grief, so group members will no doubt experience some of that as they close this particular chapter in their grieving process. Give everyone a blank piece of paper and make sure everyone has a pencil. Ask each group member to write his or her name at the top of the page.

Now ask everyone to pass their papers one person to the right. That person will write a message of comfort, a prayer thought, or a word of encouragement—a message, prayer, or encouragement intended for the person whose name appears at the top of the page. After a minute or so, ask everyone to again pass the papers to the right and repeat the process.

Continue until everyone has written on everyone else's paper and all group members have their own papers back. Finally, read **2 Thessalonians 3:16** as a blessing before you dismiss the group:

May the Lord of peace Himself give you peace at all times and in every way. The Lord be with all of you. Amen.

❖